ALSO BY JORDAN DAVIS

PREVIOUS BOOK PUBLICATIONS

Million Poems Journal (Faux Press, 2003)

CHAPBOOKS

POD: poems on demand (Greying Ghost, 2011)

From Orange to Pink (Fewer & Further Editions, 2009)

A Winter Magazine (Situations, 2002)

Yeah, No (Detour, 2001)

Poem on a Train (Barque, 1998)

Upstairs (Barque, 1997)

A Little Gold Book (Golden, 1995)

EDGE BOOKS

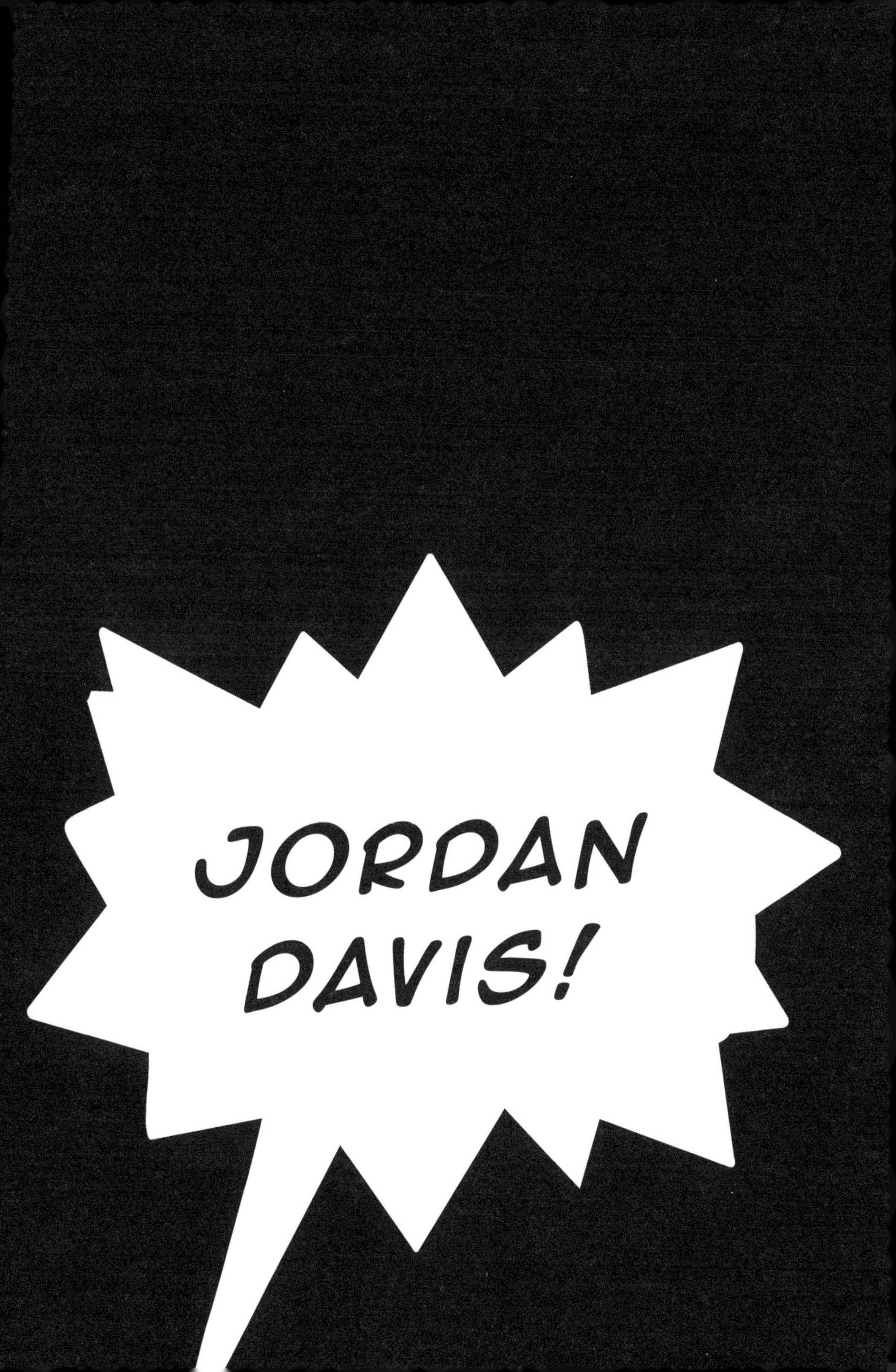
JORDAN DAVIS!

EDGE BOOKS

P.O. BOX 25642

GEORGETOWN STATION

WASHINGTON, D.C. 20027

AERIALEDGE@GMAIL.COM

FOR **HENRY**

TO READ WHEN HE'S OLDER

FOR **JAMES**

WHEN HE FEELS LIKE IT

AND FOR **ROGER**

IF HE'S OUT THERE

I

DRONE

3

OTTERS

5

SHELL GAME

6

NOTES ON COPYRIGHT

21

MOSTLY READ THE LUNA MOTH

26

NARRAGANSETT

28

IRA WILL NOT BE ATTENDING THE MEETING

29

THE SHOUTING

30

THE HOVEL

32

CITY AS

33

THE MOON IS MOVING

34

WHEN I WAS THE SUBJECT

35

II

MY ORHAN VELI

47

MANYOSHU BLUES

64

III

KEEP THE DRUMS AT YOUR MOM'S

73

NOT NOTHING NEVER NO

75

FEELING NUMB

77

THE FACILITY FINDER

79

THE IDEA ITSELF

80

HA HA ONLY SERIOUS

82

MY HOSTILITY

83

MY TWIN

84

TWENTY BLOCKS

96

FROM THE TWENTIETH FLOOR

98

A MILLION RANDOM DIGITS

100

LOOK DOWN

104

THE THROAT

107

NEW WORDS 1939–1945

112

I

DRONE

What frees the hand
from its patronym
is a terrible swift word,

not a life-drawing class.
How much worse than being talked about
is it to be painted?

The yelps continue—
bless the hand for it is non-conceptual
and variable in its uses;

neither am I content
with fig pinions o'er my crotch.
Lo the trucks arrive

and I, having had the trees to copy
and the roaches and the rats
am thankful I guess.

I am bells and ghosts
throwing my feet at the tireless street,
I am not tired I am shining

no one brings me what I want
shouting and whistling
in the hallways and a breeze

coming in the window

OTTERS

So much of poetry
is filled with stuff
that fills poetry. Also,
this stuff is so often
arranged in a way
stuff is arranged
in poetry. We ought
to get together
and steal time
from our jobs
to put stuff
in poetry
that wasn't
there before,
and arrange it
in a way stuff
isn't usually arranged.

Click here to watch
a video of otters
floating, holding hands.

SHELL GAME

The material, a cut on my knuckle.
We go out to the shell game
but it's a liability
dressed up as a pork chop.
I am bleeding from my birthstone.
McGriddle, what's that on the radar
to starboard? Can we just open
and close this vacuum door in peace?
The peanuts go flying.
Money is covered with sad faces.

The presidents walk across the flag.
That's part of my strategy
but the best dream I ever had
waits in a canister, safe from mites.
Capacity to free associate
divorced entirely from will to understand.
Excitement misfired.
Love, covetous love
pouring from my heart
like goo on walls in a movie.
I don't watch that kind of movie.

Yes, that's fine. Just stay awake
and keep talking
until the colors line up on the cube . . .
The death instinct, "Nobody's going
to tell me what to do" in hot pants.
No. Yes. No. Yes. The opposite
of broken is sex. Maybe.

Everyday life in a poem, a headline—
it proves kidnappers haven't killed it.
My heart just wanted to feel safe
so I created some great drama
based on a movie from before I was born.
I wanted to feel love. Then I did.
I do. I said that in front of a judge.

The bad guy is back in town!
Too late, though—everybody died
of boredom. But you know, a true villain
needs only his own estimation
to thrive. In cartoons
enemies are merely competitive
spoilsports. Here,
in this Père Lachaise de l'Ennui
we toast the Widow Time
and her entirely actualized indifference.

Bless her.

You're wearing your brains
at a jaunty angle, eh, old bean?
Or as a finer maker put it,
your smarts are on your garment.
If I wanted to know how magnets work
I'd reread *Lord Jim*. Meanwhile
the more gorgeous of the two
tries on a rhetoric
that, like any good television comedian,
consists mainly of shouting.

The corollary to never turn
your back on the ocean is
always size up the opposition
while walking away smiling.
Rod Smith calls it
"the wanting-it tax." Owen Barfield
says it's what's wrong with religion.
Pamela Anderson and I
were voted "Class class"
at my high school. At that time,
the actress who shares her name
had not yet been discovered.

Feeling comes through in writing;
this is what Wilde meant
about bad writing and sincerity—
sincerity and irony are taming influences
both. Feeling is on the move,
arrow on string. When I see
that a reflex remark is about
to strike you, I turn abstract.
You in turn feel my absence
for the submerged aggression it is.
I think Wilde would have gotten a kick
out of Freud, don't you?

Spontaneity and carelessness—
not the same. The teacher
said something about meteorite craters
forming volcanoes. If we have to have
a standard greeting as a culture,
can it be "What up," and not
"All praise to the truth?" Thanks.
Thanks too for bringing
this ultimate crumb cake.
True, I am developing a belly,
but also I feel compassion,
the heft of dough, the shirr
of flour, butter and sugar.

Keep your eye on the bent card.
All the cards are bent, actually.
All right then, keep your eye.
The ball is there then it's not.
My son shows me the plastic cups,
the miniature poms, then starts
stacking. YouTube it: Cup stacking.
It's a sport, like moonwalking
or electioneering.

I don't care about

the general assembly. It has gold leaf

like a church, and two abstract

bacteria flank its unsanitary earphones.

But the things they talk about there!

Those are not things they're people.

Small arms in small hands.

It takes 3,000 hours to tend a paddy.

Whatever you're looking for,

buy it the day after Christmas.

And as for flood insurance, forget it.

The people they talk about, though,

are halfway to thank you. Always with us.

I'm opening a bar called "Liquidity Trap."
A bookstore named "Carpe Diem."
"Vanity, All Is Vanity"—health club.
Actually that'll do for pretty much anything,
pig. No, not you. I meant that language
policeman behind you. Scratch an American,
sniff a cop. Smoke a bowl. Feel a mop.
Scratch an American, win a lifetime
all expenses charged back to you
trip to the front. Scratch an American,
find your way through the smoke.

Oh is it.

Is that so.

Well I never.

You don't say.

On the contrary.

Always a pleasure.

How may I help you.

That's what she said.

It's lovely to see you.

That's not what I heard.

Germany's outline on a map—
a bird or a skull. I'd never
noticed it before, never
imagined it onto stones
or shells on walks as I do
with Nevada, Delaware, Africa.
New York Snoopy. California
telephone. Washington
sideburns. DC diamond.
I just blocked it out.
Now I see it. A bird or a skull.

Baffle baffle baffle, disclose
baffle. Baffle baffle baffle
disclose, baffle baffle. Baffle
disclose, baffle disclose,
baffle baffle baffle disclose
baffle. Baffle. Baffle.

NOTES ON COPYRIGHT

Hoarding knowledge. Some do it.

The impulse to hoard knowledge appears to be ingrained / hard-wired / fundamental.

J. Edgar Hoover / Dick Cheney / leveraging private information / everyone.

Scientology / the audit.

The mosaic doctrine—no way to know what information will be important therefore must restrict access.

Loose lips sink ships—clear and present danger—alien and sedition acts.

Competitive advantage / trade secrets.

Collyer Bros / Memoir found in a bathtub / Keep this forever / Delete.

Hoarders / Pickers / Storage Wars / Antique Roadshow

Nicholson Baker / Robert Darnton—digitization as premise for destruction of books. (Báez.)

Secrecy causes lying / Hersh.

Security clearances throttle the flow of information upwards.

Volumes of data exceed the ability to filter, for a time—

Search is described as algorithms and indexes.

Capture danger—copies of a single version of the entire set will replace the massively redundant and various multiple sets—

The bonus incentive applied to the management of renewable resources.

Knowledge and the bonus incentive.

Knowledge managed in the same way on an annual, quarterly, monthly, weekly, intraday basis.

Hoarding / social impulse. (Followers / friends.)

Need to belong / to feel superior / special.

Having thousands of friends or followers / millions of uniques —the bonus incentive applied to . . . ?

Broadcast media logic / the individual.

Granular time. Silica gel

The social impulse and the algorithm / George Harrison's reply to Victor Spinetti: "I don't think it's very likely that we will go on. The law of averages is against it."

Then: "She's a drag. A well-known drag. We turn the sound down on her and say rude things."

Hope ⟶ self-protection ⟶ frontierism ⟶ go west.

"Took a left turn at Greenland."

The new frontier / opening of the field / sub-Saharan Africa.

Assume that living authors will limit the searchable universe of books to the public domain.

Trademarking a grain / patenting a genome.

Could anyone ever pre-empt the public domain.

How much storage would it take to hold standard-format documents of all existing public domain material?

Not in the cloud—on an appliance. (Assume that over time as with all public goods there will be a privatization.)

An archive pre-loaded onto a device subsidized by the settle of search with the living holders of copyright.

Patriot act / library searches / our reading is not your property.

It will do no good to put these devices in the hands of children if their parents have no time to read along and talk with them.

Learning and civilization / inertia.

Data is fragile. Civilization.

If works can be retained and instantly available forever, what about the intellectual equivalent of estate tax repeal—infinite copyright.

Flarf / plagiarism / selection.

The narrative of the data deluge is that unexpected narratives will emerge.

A full-disclosure world overloads the shame/guilt circuits.

The timeline. Misdemeanors as evidence of personal development —a citizenship of safely catchable, controllable criminals.

MOSTLY READ THE LUNA MOTH

The savor of mango is unlike
toothsome papay. My son takes
my hand and brings me
into the classroom; Fluffy
is absent and unremarked-upon

and in his place, two butterflies
use tentatively in a sentence.
One, he explains, is a boy and
the other one lays the eggs,
I counted the dots, is a girl.

Why do boys not feed babies?
He reaches to pull his shirt open
and I ask him, did you ever see
a baby eat broccoli? a ham sandwich?
Someday I will tell him

food is an unpleasant subject
for poems, but today I am concerned
with biology. I am a science kid,
he says on the platform. Where'd
he hear that. I know where the one

about men nursing came from.
Seeing myself tell that story
I feel like California's
poisoned groundwater and remember
how much work it is to be real.

Someone told you men can give milk,
but men don't. What about moms and dads
who don't have children? Those are
called men and women. He says
"Oh" a lot. It's immediate

and it lags into the next moment
and is quiet, what the teachers call
a zone of proximal delay. Without
this apparent lull there is only
brilliance and potential. With it

I get to keep a faith
in the unguessable next.

NARRAGANSETT

The complete sentence narrates a satisfying process.
It closes and opens like a clam.
I take a knife to the sentence and start my evening at the raw bar.
It is hard work, and the sentences would prefer to be in the ocean.
I would rather be a patron of this establishment.
Someone over my shoulder
would rather know I am going to continue to put up with his stuff.
It is not a wide receiver, his stuff. It is his development,
which is gradual. It involves testing me. Sometimes
these tests take the form of imperatives. Drive onto the boat!
The boat would rather be en route to Maine.
It is an ambitious ferry. My knife wishes to whittle patterns
into the enormous picnic table. Art does not narrate.

IRA WILL NOT BE ATTENDING THE MEETING

When working on a small scale
He is practicing a gesture.
So much of life is practicing gestures.
So much of living is evaluating
those around you for signs of damage.

Now it is night, morning's a blink away.
Sleep is sometimes thought of
as an avalanche of repair gnomes
that attends your pit stop.
Would that we were sleeping now!

Viable alternatives will be reviled
until the point of no return is passed.
The only reasonable course of action
is to look for sizeable flotsam,
redo the resume, learn a martial art.

THE SHOUTING

Such rich
attention
to every flaw,

a memory
like shale
for trapped words.

Anything spoken
at any volume
is shouting.

Hello an affront,
no hello
an affront too—

a pinned-up feeling
in the chest
as if a nude
flashed on the screen.

This object
emotion
keeps making me
say its name.

THE HOVEL

I'm in awe
of the appetite
my quiet neighbor has—

the feeling someone is talking to you
about something important
is half bread.

The bank on the corner in its red and blue
has one face to us and then its side
as the train rounds and descends,

the initials scratched in the glass
shine over a wet street
then the city houses where the ground
takes in the cars.

CITY AS

Tape down the white sky
for coffee-colored music,

make pharaohs of prairies
bend drawings to drum.

Yes make them.

Make them look up
their mistakes

on the sides of buildings.

THE MOON IS MOVING

High above the subway
And the airplanes
It starts above the Bronx
And finishes in New Jersey
It goes behind the rooftops
As the bus goes down the avenue
It moves over the courtyard
And shines on you
As you dream of flying
It starts out pink
And ends up yellow
Every night there is less
Or more of it
Until it's round like a clock
As when you turn to look
The second hand seems to stop
Just so the moon
The moon is moving

WHEN I WAS THE SUBJECT

How we or anything exists
is cranky extravagance,
forthright New Year's hibiscus chaos.

O note card on the floor
I can't speak to you
like someone at the end
of a nine foot wall
but if you have a birthday
I will sing to you.

Flashing Christmas lights
is it your yes that's many-colored
or like the tree in silhouette
is it no?

I am the love of a pullet
for the hoseman
which shines whiter
than a new refrigerator.

I am the color
of the sweater the woman

for whom I have many
little feelings wears
(my eyes are that color).

Candle squiggle on ceiling
copper connects its way
across the room
as a woman whose
neckline is
a stone necklace
lifts the shotglass
candle to light
her smoke—

look deep into the street,
a glass of glass.

The cat you have
to let come to you.

The arc of the moral
universe bends toward
who plainly say
warm day surrounded beauty wants
catfish in restaurant meanings.

The song of plaid paper
and plastic around roses
is *step all the way in.*

Kid screams her head
can't take my eyes off of you
trumpet solo in Times Square.

Bystander camera crew
looking for the mole of the week.

Governance all afternoon
and context in the evening
set their tuning forks
on a sleeping head,

graffiti on shoulder strap—
imagine being that far gone
they could actually tag *you.*

For a dollar I'll
tell you a poem:
Bad career move.

Coconut oil out of control—
O no! Symmetry . . .

Sleepy woman at a payphone:
"My love never mind my love
it's your love that means . . ."
She going to make it? Reeling,
counting her change.

New poem
come up from
the earth
the south
the minors . . .

What are the questions
anything asks:

Education or sex?
Laundry or painting?
Sadness or weight gain?
Computers or square feet?
Laughter or knowing looks?
Quasars or pinatas?
Carbon-dating or Bichon Frises?
Restocking the wilds or hovering overhead?
Companion volume or appellate court?
Deep or homely?

Quiet or common?
Reply or sonogram?
Wanton abandonment or annuities?
Justice or victory?
Tragedy or periplum?
Arabic or cellular?

What funny thing
has the caffeine
persuaded you
I need to see?

If I had forty youths to give this art
each of them youngly angry and amused
I'd relegate the sidewalk sidelong crush
to one or two and with the balance make
plays, movies, ways that words move people, light

match-sulfur
then tears in the eyes.

In constant danger of eye-contact
not that anything you want is a rockstar.

Small stuff or clue?

Remember liking the word constellation?
And I was a stranger to you.

The keys receipts candy wrappers in
the unwashed clothes of the dead.

Those people
locked in game.

Would I could need
what I was thinking
like I need a thing.

O so-what, do you ease
an anxious smile into its case?

So-what zipper on a tight lace boot,
so-what blue jeans on old people,
the crowds massed
for the celebration
of the year of so-what.

To so-what I send my resume;
I show up for the interview
in my interview suit,
am casual but poised

and so-what and I
get along I get
the job!

O so-what,
we go walking
where the oxygen flows
and nothing knows
either of us.

You think I smile
because anybody
notices but
laughter as insulation
is all this life
sparkles
to the order of
we like you.

I am in love
does not function as
an emotional declarative
the way
So I was getting ready
for my father to die
does.

This doesn't have to do
with truth value or even
meaningful probability.

Whether true or false
so I was getting ready
is unarguable.

Anxiety like love a state
of looking for an object.

I'm so far from the border
of being in love and not
being in love.

Lightning is my cello of
the person-place continuum.

The ice sheet standing near
my head is noticed.

The things I notice are
not the things I think about
or feel they're what
get sucked through the
hole I punch in time.

When I see a man sitting
on a stool in front of bricks
I know I am the firing squad.

The tough guy voice
I parodied to get it
to take me over—

doorways
grinning as stupidly as I do.

And when the energy has
almost finished going
through we can work
out a few things

without the sharp
points sticking out.

MY ORHAN VELI

WHAMMO!

Everything hits at once—
Daylight
Sky
Blue.
Whammo!
Smoke off the ground
Shoots
Buds
Fruit.

Zwack! Thhppt.
Girls and boys!
Roads
Fields
Cats
People!
Boom!
Love!
Pow!
Joy.

OUT OF TOWN

Red and swollen bumps at the ends of things
mean to make some nice days.
A woman out of town
face down on the grass
in the sun
means the same thing
in her red and swollen breasts and belly.

FOR ISTANBUL

APRIL

Can't write poems
when you're in love—
can't not write them
in April.

WISHES AND THE PAST

What you want changes
and so does the past.
How does anybody keep going
when it's always gray?

INSECTS

Stop thinking
just follow what you need!
That's how the insects do it.

INVITATION

My door's open.
Come by
when it's so nice out
you can't take it.

ALLER ET RETOUR

I watch the boat go—
Can't jump in after it,
and men don't cry, dammit.

SOME DAYS

Some days I get myself together
and take off in the smell of nets
hauled on deck between islands
in the wake of the trawlers.

Some places I've been
flowers boom when they bloom;
They even leave a smoke trail.

The seagulls let you know
they feel it in every feather.

Some days I turn completely blue,
some days the sun hits me from all sides,
some days I have no choice but surrender.

LIFE

Life could drive you crazy—
Night! Stars! The breeze
coming off this flower-covered tree.

INDOORS

The window's great—
Along with your four walls, you get birds going by.

THE OCEAN

In my bed in the morning
I can tell without getting up
that the boats going by
are shipping watermelons.

The sea likes to reflect light
across my ceiling;
It's trying to get
a rise out of me.

Seaweed and fishing poles
pulled up on shore
remind the children who live here
of nothing.

MORNING

Covering the lake's face with my hand
I stare at the clouds
as the camel hurries to get to the horizon
before the sun comes up.

MAHMUT THE MOOCHER

What do I do?
Every night while you're asleep
I paint the sky blue.

When the sea tears,
who do they get to sew it up?
Yours truly.

I moonlight daydreaming—I dream there's
a head in my head,
a belly in my belly,
a foot in my foot.

You have a better idea?

POEM WITH A RAPID SHAKE

I woke up and the sun was in my heart—
I was ruffled and shaking rapidly
like birds and leaves in a crisp breeze,
all of me a-flutter.

That's me—birds and leaves.
Birds
and leaves.

ESTATES BOUGHT AND SOLD

Estates bought and sold
and converted into stars.
If music be the food of life—
Great! I love music.

Poems written and told
and traded for estates,
estates traded for scraps of music.
Why can't I just be a fish in a bottle of scotch?

PAVED POEMS

I

I love
to see a new horizon
when the building by the road's
in ruins.

II

I wish I was a kid
with the others on the curb
watching the steamroller give off smoke
and move on.

III

The huge noise of it
sounds to a friend of mine
like motorboats
showing off across the harbor.

IV

Is this what poets are for,
I wonder—
To stare at the old ripped up road
and predict wet shiny pavement?

JUST GREAT

Great is the color of tea
before the day's gotten going
and the sunlight's just warming up.
Great weather.
Great kid who brought the cup.
Great tea.

EROL GUNEY'S CAT

Poem expressing Erol Guney's cat's
point of view in springtime
on the problems of society:

Give me a big Tom and some liver
and I'm set.
Damn straight.

Poem addressing Erol Guney's cat's
impending motherhood:

What did you expect,
going down to the street to enjoy the spring?
It's all right, now you get
to lie around
practicing thinking and worrying.

MY BED

Every night in bed
I lie and think of her.
As long as I love her
I'll love this bed too.

STILL THERE?

I did notice your heart beating
as we tried to finish putting the kite together.
I didn't know then I could tell you how I felt.
Are you still alive?

WHAT WAS THAT?

Was I really supposed to feel this,
lose sleep
and stare distractedly into the air?
Never even noticing
the destruction of the downtown Armory?
Are the predestinationists somehow onto something?

PEOPLE

Not all the time
but when you make it clear

you don't know who I am,
I want to be in mom's lap
looking at you
the way I looked at people
before I knew anything about them.

SUNDAY NIGHT

Yes, now I am dressed badly
but when I pay off my debts
I'll get some fine clothes
and you will still not love me.
However, when I walk down your street
dressed in my respectable-man disguise
I won't be carrying you around
in my heart like this, thank God.

BAR

Now that it's over,
why go back to the bar
where I used to drink
and think of her?

MASTURBATION

Drunk, I called you,
my left hand,
my old flame.

GOOD AND SAD

It might have gotten on my nerves,
loving people,
if love
hadn't taught me
to get good and sad, and stay that way.

TEMPORARY INSANITY

Over her at last!
And the world is full of girls.
A new silk shirt,
a hot bath,
a clean shave.
It's spring, in peacetime;
I'm in the sun.
I'm in the street, everybody's happy.
Me too.

QUIET ENJOYMENT

What's going on so late
in the house up on the hill?
What do they need all the lights on for,
conversation? Parcheesi?
Invoicing?

If it's talking they're doing,
is it the war or the economy?
Maybe nothing's going on—
Kids in bed, dad watching the game,
mom among piles of fabric.

I feel funny staring and speculating—
It's not just none of my business,
it may well be unsayable,
unknowable,
whatever they're up to up there.

HEADACHE

The road may be lovely
the night may not be long—
Your body gets heavy
but your headache goes strong.

If I go inside at one
I can come back out at three—
These clothes and shoes are mine
and the streets (so far) are free.

TRAVELING

I

When you travel,
stars talk to you;
They try hard
to make you sad.

II

When you're drunk
it feels good to whistle—
It doesn't sound as good
on a train.

MY SHADOW

I've had it carrying you around
on the end of my shoe—
We need some space for a while,
and to see other people.

I'M SPECIAL

The sun doesn't make me sick
and I don't care about April
or the almond tree covered in flowers.
It's not going to kill me,
and what if it does, how bad
can it be to die in the sun?
Every spring I'm a year younger,
and more deeply in love.
What's death going to do to me?
I'm special. I have a different problem.

THE ROAD FROM THE DEATH FACTORY

Hey, when we're dead
and it's quitting time at the Death Factory
if the road home goes downhill
wouldn't that be an improvement?

RELIEF

You say you've had it
with getting hungry
angry
lonely
and tired.

Give me back my shovel when you're done digging!

NOPE

You don't hear me talking
about my problems because I don't know how!
It's not that they're not terrible,
I can think of a few people I'd wish them on.
And it's not a sentimental problem like a broken heart—
Nope. And it isn't exactly that I have to work at a job . . .
It's something, though.

A big impossible something.

SUICIDE

If only there were some way
to make it even look mysterious.
As it is people won't be able to keep from saying things like
"love" or "depression" or even worse "too poor"—
The only way to emphasize "none of the above"
is to keep going.

THE LYING BIRDS

Coat, trust me,
The birds are lying to you.
You're the only one for me.

Please believe me:

The birds say this every year.

Don't listen to them, coat. Please.

GUEST

A low-grade anxiety shot my day to hell yesterday,

and two packs of cigarettes had no effect on it.

I tried to write my way out of it—mistake.

Got a decent tone out of a violin

(decent for a first try, anyway),

went out into the street

and looked in on a backgammon game,

sang badly (on purpose),

caught enough flies to fill a rent envelope,

and then, goddammit!

I wound up here.

HEADING TO THE FRONT

Marine recruitment poster boy packed off for Syria,

come back in mint condition, ok?

With that printer's ink smell of boot polish,

I know they used foundation to make you that matte

but is that mascara peeking out under the full dress hat?

O intense and sad advertisement for war.

LIKE US

Do you think a tank gets a hard-on
when it enters the REM stage of sleep?
Is it likely that an airplane daydreams
when it sits empty to be refueled?

Do you suppose gas masks get bored
chanting monotonously
under the full moon?

Aren't machine guns probably as decent
as your average, regular, stand-up guy?

LONELINESS

Until you've been truly by yourself
you don't know how scary quiet is,
how you talk to yourself in every mirror
looking for a living being—
Sorry, you just don't.

MANYOSHU BLUES

They can put fire in a bag
But they can't bring you back

My wife would wrap around me
Like seaweed swaying back and forth

—I waited for you by the lake
   And the dew got me all wet.
—Don't make me jealous of the dew!

As I shoveled the plow slop
From the end of the drive,
Trees cracking, ten in all,
And chickadees singing for dinner—
Collaborators with the shovel scrape
On the backing track
Of my blues.

Rascal! Why isn't that the name
Of a comic book supervillain.
Maybe it is. If only there were
A way to read in all the world's libraries
Wherever we are, and remedy
Our ignorance.

How many men, when I was a boy,
Looked like rocks.
I wonder why I don't see them any more.
Where did they go?
Did the process that makes men rocks just stop?

The ruined castle—
They unfriended it.

I know that this absence
Is temporary. Life, also,
Is temporary. The next time I see you
I will put you in handcuffs
And read you your rights.

So much better
Than committing more jackass bullshit
Is this sake.

If there were a form of germ warfare
That could stop everybody from writing,
I think I'd still prefer a cup of sake.

Come live with me.
We'll be like two ducks.

I like when I see you in dreams,
Even when you tell me I don't taste the same.

Stupid old servant, to take my hawk without asking!
'He flew into the clouds.' Stupid! Stupid!

My hawk soars.
It gives me great pleasure
To think of it
Tearing across the sky

After a duck.
In my room I close the door
Close my eyes
And just think about it.

Oh my God!
I better do something good—
I mean, I'm a man.

The fountain of youth—
It's whitewater
And you have to kayak it.

So, this is it.
Lying like a dog by the side of the road.
Figures.

That's human life for you—
Caught like a bird.

It's a good thing they didn't close down the terminal—
When I heard your plane had landed
I ran over to the walkway—
My closed up bookbag tucked under the bench.

When I'm with you
I get so stupid
I want to live a thousand years.

I trust myself
Like a big ship.

Since she was eight
They've kept her hidden.
Two boys fight over her—
With swords. One wins.
Oh shit, she thinks.
No fucking way
Does that oblige me
To do anything.
It does? Fuck that shit,
She says, and dies.

The snow shining on the palace-court—
And outside the palace, too—
I could look at it all day
And never see everything turn green.

I didn't think anybody else was out on the bay,
Then I heard oars, new moon.

Everywhere I go, the same flowers—
This analogy does not apply to one's mother.

I'll never forget the words of my mother and father—
'See you soon.'

I say my prayers,
Load my gun,
Hit the road.

I wish that, instead of turning you into a cloud,
They could make a jewel of you
For someone special to wear. They can?
Talk about careful what you wish for!

Nice hatchet!
Let's see if it floats.

—Sell my dragonfly scarf
   And buy a horse, husband—
   I hate to see you walk to work.

—But if I have a horse, dear bride,
   One of us will still have to walk.
   Let's walk on the rocks together.

.

KEEP THE DRUMS AT YOUR MOM'S

Orange oil trebuchet'd over the top of the cubicle.

I am staring at a lump of clay shaped like a fathead fish.

The prism on my desk, my fake industry award,

sends its seam on a lucite diagonal.

If I were to teach middle school math

I'd want to review my proofs.

The stack of trimmed letterhead doesn't light up to see me,

doesn't it know I'm an addict?

If you want to use ProTools on me,

if you want to Photoshop my face, I'm ready.

"Unknown number" keeps flashing on my phone.

The white bird steps sideways in the melt.

Someone sends me a hate search.

The sleep of a barmaid is white as a robot

and all the perimeter's a butterfly bush;

I huddle under the lilacs.

Impossible for an individual and yet

now come the stray billion diatoms carving out prime numbers in
    the slush.

The horse song which is a veto of all that is probable

on the left edge of the reading room,

the song of no experience, comes for the pale tray—

it takes a button from my coat and measures it in farads.

A tree street bends in its matching shifts

intimating slavery and pendulums,

a rocking in the hips, overexposed film.

NOT NOTHING NEVER NO

Sleepy sweater wearer,
making maximum wage for a middleman in Lodi,
playing bass in a dive bar in Little Rock,
baiting the contender for a bit of rope-a-dope
in Shreveport,
it is the American way to love names.
What we repeat
teaches us rhetoric
and calls it music.
It sincerely hopes to bed us,
and maybe the beach
will come right up to the library
with an invitation for us to grow up already.
What do you say. Up for
some growing? The artist
goes barreling down a context.
He has buffed his concept to a lustre.
Mayhap you will join him at the AMF
for a few frames. Maybe he will tell you
what you are dying to hear, which is
neither here nor there. This
peculiar unpleasant space called poetry,
for sooth, no worse than a nightclub

and no better than a house on fire.
Ah, said the American, that cannot be helped.
Ah, said the American, we must be ruled
by the wealthy inept. It is our heritage
and birthright—all citizens
are entitled to feel contempt
for their leaders, and by extension,
for themselves. You too, sexy.

FEELING NUMB

Overrated, generally, though there are contexts . . .
Behind every great fortune there is a great context—

tingling feelings' cousin.
The stereo sits waiting for me to light up its robot mouth.

I passed the hamburger stand
with five dollars in my pocket.

I tested the limits of my vulnerability
then decided to start loving

the light pummelling upward through the notch
between the pencils and the throb

of all these filthy meanings a mayor
can't abandon simply by giving a film crew a permit . . .

To the ramparts, he shouted like a child
and we admired his absolutist gusto

until it was clear he was incapable of following orders
and moreover would not rest until we were dead.

Free spirits lobbing
kits at the standing water I mean kites

at the breeze off
the long-turned tide.

There was much to feel
and yet we'd signed on

for too big a supply
of these moods—

this legendary first person
we'd heard so much about.

THE FACILITY FINDER

I was pleased to discover America.
It cheered me up to hear everybody else fighting.
When I finally gave my hostility a name
I started cleaning up after it like a proper pet.
It felt great to make a fuzzy electrical sound.
Holding my place on line with the book
of my one thousand doodles gave me
inordinate feelings of pride. Or ordinate, maybe.
The sun making wavy lines on the roofs
of the parking lot, the waves making
a glint-covered sunset on the roof of my heart,
the roofs keeping me my accustomed level
of damp, it all meant one thing: tautology
is the energy source of the future, and you
are the one I want beside me in the vehicle,
our hands on each other's knees,
shouting our heads off to the music
recorded on this obsolete medium
as a low-cost way to express our earliest vibes.

THE IDEA ITSELF

Men in tophats
chasing cash on the breeze—

to know the truth
and watch the world ignore it

fight it in fact
with all its paper . . .

The gold doors of the vault
protect some old comedy.

The desk has nothing on it.
Well, a Guinness . . .

A good likeness
for an origin myth.

I put the cake up to my chin
filled with love for my countrymen.

The lines of the factory guide the plane
into a mirrored quilted space

lined with vases of roses,
the very limousine of heaven.

Individuals are hard to find
even with the armbands;

I love the French for thinking so
and pity their bad luck.

We live among childish rubrics
and a pizza oven

vacant so long squirrels
have claimed it in the name of gorp.

HA HA ONLY SERIOUS

I cry every day.
I wake up and look over at the books
lying across your side of the bed.
I make bread because I have to knead something.

My heart feels heavy
like I dropped it on myself.
I am spinning a cocoon of paper.
When I emerge I'll have wings of dust.

Every second in this city
everyone judges everyone else.
And themselves too.
They only give gold medals to people who take them.

A mockingbird stays up with me.
Bird, you're a little ahead of your entrance.
Come help me wash away all the flour.
Sing me the song of the garbage trucks and cops.

MY HOSTILITY

I am drawn to it in others.
It is a vast and disembodied headache
I massage and abandon,
a pilgrim with a lantern.
There I could be a girl, a blue light
and no interest in the dreary *after* photos.
It seeks a pace to kill a horse
but lives like a tiger in an old zoo
reciting choice bits of On *the Waterfront*
while mentally photostatting the blacklist.

MY TWIN

Framing tale goes here.
Something about losing ten pounds
when I stopped eating all the bread I bake.
Whatever. You understand.
My twin watches a movie.
My twin watches a movie during work
at the theater
he snuck into. Afterward
he calls, "Where the hell am I?"
I care a lot about his mood.

At your age, absolutely.
Prove it in colors.
Take purple scissor steps
believing in the silence of the grocery
weeds love concrete
speeches. A plastic smell.
Blue and white. She smiles all at once
and I'm happy for her
but I don't understand.

Crazy pizza. Shell game.
Twelve midnights. It's dark
in the living room and it smells
like plastic. Favorite color: blue.
Favorite substance: gluten.
But everybody's breaking.
It makes me laugh, like college students
at the news the city's being bombed.
They don't understand. Neither does
my twin. I love to look at her.

I have great love for my twin.
When he says to carry his bag
I do it, and when he says
to clean up his purslane
and repair the carburetors,
and when he says he's depressed
I arrange some aerobic moodlight.
I feel trapped. I crash my bike.
I read every story in the Times
every day. I wake up with a hard-on.

Take it easy with that power hose.
There in the outdoor furniture
three or four conversations taking place,
At least one of them is serious.
Do you like graphic design?
Is that a dremel?
The questions are local
but the answers are off the rack. The hook.
That part's not so relaxing.
It has too many children
and nothing surprises it anymore.

Stacks of newspapers,
research documents
and keepsakes. Binder clips.
Shortness of breath.
Subcutaneous nodules.
An eight-gallon reservoir
that wicks up into the planter
while you're *en vacances*.
Eagles nesting in the gargoyles.
That person were a kind of solution.

Once I thought we might be astronomers.
This was during a science special
about extinction via massive cosmic ray bursts
or the collision of galaxies.
"What if our star is a binary
and we just don't know it yet?" I said.
My twin muttered at his fretboard,
got up, and closed his door behind him.
We actually only have one room.
Soon I saw smoke rolling under the door,
the river rising in its banks.

Leaning to the left, literally.
A standing lamp makes me happy
as bread. As dough in the hands
of my happiness. An alarm.
A toast, to the king
and his taste for alarms.
Short strokes, cross-hatched.
Idealized. Bonkers. Louie Louie.

Is not afraid of death.
Is not afraid of "is."
Zero equal sign passive voice
pornography. Absolute zero
is not afraid
for you to feel more alive than it.
My twin tears out a page.
Causes pleasure being torn.
To make you feel,
my twin is into that.

More sad than I the snow's done,

Magician Pie Tin. My twin.

Fox and geese, get your gun.

Piggie move up, Jacob and Rachel.

Oh the feelings a twin can have.

A twin can have them. My twin.

My feelings are obscure

and all A's. Oakland.

Modesto Bee Minuses. The Garden Grove

Handwriting Evaluation Day.

My twin stole the rubber stamps.

I stayed up writing a report on the sphinx.

Won't let me tell jokes.
My twin makes the rules.
The shell game on Canal.
Contaminated? My twin smokes up.
Addiction, pregnancy, bankruptcy,
my twin laughs at suicide
because it's upside down.
She's kind of fucked up.
I don't let myself think it
but she insists.
"Look, look at the numbers."

I wait. I wait for my twin to say something
the way I've noticed he always waits
for me. Nothing. Silence. Zero. The moon.
Maybe he isn't waiting for me after all—
that can't possibly be it. Can it?

TWENTY BLOCKS

Bicycles passing the backed-up cars,
a cat stepping along the puddled rift
between the curb's metal lip and road,

woman after woman turning up somewhere
on the scale of having-made-an-effort,
while us men, who can tell, really.
(Part of how we keep doing the telling.)

If only I smoked, then I'd have a reason
to breathe in this dirty air more often.
Up in that narrow tower, I turn away
from the obvious symbolism

looking down when all the other exits
are being repainted, but down here
I keep getting the feeling conversation

could break out at any time. As soon as
I mention the physical world I notice
all these bodies breathing, moving along,
and what about sex, anyway. It's good,

right? Yes I would give it many stars.
And—once you start talking about it,
it takes its share of the taffy

which is all of it. Caffeinated heartbeat,
beesting, freefall, safeword, linebreak,

you are more gorgeous than an afternoon
but what they are interested in
is whether you can raise money.

Prove that much, and then maybe
we'll deal you in on a policy discussion.

FROM THE TWENTIETH FLOOR

I can take the elevator downstairs for a soda, or I can get a
glass of water from the cooler. Not a glass, a plastic tumbler;
not the rigid kind, but a soft one with a rounded lip, water
droplets adhering along the cascade. I am taking a break
from drafting a memo for an executive vice president;
in Iraq a convoy of contractors is moving along, looking
busy, waiting to be shot at, bombed, and driven into. "I really
liked it at first," I overhear the actress who temps say
from her chair in the copy/mail room. I think she's referring
to the design of the org chart she's perpetually
updating. In Uganda, a rebel group made up mostly of
child soldiers destabilizes the northern regions in
a way the government either cannot control, or
will not. I've lowered my chair level with
the guest chair across from my SMED desk. My
guest, my boss, left as I took a phone call from someone on an
island off Massachusetts. The phone call is over, and no one
is sitting here with me, but I've left the chair down even as
I strain my shoulders typing from below. That's better.
I can control the chair. I can vote
in government elections. What else. I can
keep paying attention, keep feeling something,
keep talking, keep learning how people acquire

power. Or just keep clicking around. In Bermuda,
an authoritarian from England links
to a grammar stickler from Lesotho. The stickler lives in Paris.
Sometimes the stickler just observes local variations of idiom.
These kinds of sentences I feel as free of threat.
So much communication seems to me
intended as fear-inspiring threat. Sometimes I'm
distorting my experience, sometimes not. It is quiet
in the office: a little typing, a phone conversation in a distant
cubicle, a click, a cough, something plastic being torn.

A MILLION RANDOM DIGITS

Almost surely nothing up my sleeve.
Nothing like a sleeve, for that matter.
No story, no instant winner, no glade
where the traditional "elk dance"
precedes the coronation of the flower king
and the dukes and duchesses of the forest,
no bindi manufacturer, no waterslide,
no ack ack, no Brest-Litovsk accords
and certainly no infinite monkeys
the book of only numbers
is remarkable for its persistence
and stylishness—five by five
Albers Reinhardt Mondrian Martin
have we seriously considered the grid.

Have I seen you carrying your plate
across the grassy sunlit field, stopping
abruptly and then, a moment later,
changing direction. No time for sergeants.
The pretend family. Pleasure
in the long run. Well. I've seen you
spot me across the park. I've seen
you learn a complex polyrhythm, tapping
on the drayage. I have seen you naked

and have talked when saying nothing
would have been at least as fitting,
the gibberish my neurons found meet
to haul into the light received by you
with generosity. Lomography.
Captivity narratives, earned run averages.
The walls of the underpass mosaicked
the cornsweet illusion.

Tomorrow red groovie screamed mega,
Einstein didn't fuss much with his hair,
contrast and compare starvation builds
character, race is not a factor,
and there were sunshowers and sparklers
caving in the parking lot.

The light on my chipmunk garden

But these are voicemails
when what I want what you want
is a few wrongs amended
with decimal points curving
making knock-knock jokes watermelons
the jackknifed tractor trailer
scatters on the off-ramp,

the woman across the car gums
her lips, squints closely
at the tables and charts
in this month's Lotto News.
Who's going to tell her
they call that game a "math tax."

The first recorded lottery
paid for the Great Wall of China.

We were praying in the desert
when the meteor shower
struck the enemy camp.

None of that. A tub of hot sauce.
An encounter with Human Resources.

Numbers are not letters, not words,
irony is not chance. To speak
to each plant in a loving voice.

Who wants to know if we revise?
Tell them every single night.
Tell them carbon dioxide, tell them
waves of light, of water, of sound.
Tell them I'm feeling lucky,

repeated strings appear then
a story is the intersection of
permanence and unpredictability.
The book of random numbers
allows us to conduct these tests
and all things being equal
see consistent results, a cup
of tea, an Enigma machine;

and when I'm able to breathe,
all reverting to the mean,
they'll run a Monte Carlo simulation
so I can step out for a smoke break.
When I see you, I'll cross against the light.

LOOK DOWN

The spark off the boot
makes submarine light
wave on the track walls;

a bar on the roof locks
the accordion bus
to its middle;

messengers draft
in the ambulance wake.

From the eighth floor
the cars are the size
of a four-year-old's toys;

from the twentieth
a seven-year-old
might vroom them.

When my heart hurts
I notice what's up
with my feet,

everybody walking
looking straight ahead

in a silence they don't hear—
Neither do I.

Look down

and you end up
on the ground.

The critics want the leader
not to succumb to doubts.

O slack rope
the metaphysics of morals is
for the birds

and do they navigate
by brain magnets?

Sunset light on the canals
and a precise ache in the wings

until something they've seen before
relaxes them.

People imitate when they sing
and when they don't.

The main thing is to keep talking
and also to listen

for the song
that lasts sixty years
or seventy.

Ideas of shapeliness
can't be helped:

A shoe on the floor
of Grand Central Terminal.

THE THROAT

I could never cry
until tonight
when you passed by

coughing and staring
over the bunting
you keep your anger in:

a kiss for little bear,
a nose for business.

The solution
to the next day
is an essay.

The blues rolls
down its windows,
a dance crasher;

the rabbit scurries
to the next paragraph.

This is our pleasant
present moment
built for seething;

I know that
is the catchphrase
of its hit sitcom.

The cherries here
so red they're blue
like something else
we don't mention.

In this attempt
to pass unnoticed
in the way we think
means being adored,

being the dictionary
and breaking a crystal
off the butter dish—

throwing a pot
into the bonfire
to celebrate

being on the roof
covered with amethysts.

We're hot and tired
of the regular structure
they call the beat.

They call out to us
You'll be back

You'll be the ones
We make wash our socks.

We make a lot of money
breaking down boxes
and manning the doors

and behind the curtains
the little god
is doing all the thinking.

It makes us want to dance
our way across the plural,
the shapely music
don't even speak English.

Everybody's moving to it
like it's the city
with all the jobs.

We stand around in the dark
reading the backs
and walking across
the broken windows.

Today vanishes into the side pocket
and you, practicing signals,
let me doubt the wiring.

The cartoon
on the plaster cast.

Some arrowroot yearning
calls out for an errand,

a little matter of focusing
on the throat,

of hearing in the voice
something warm like *come home*
in any weather report

and the vision it entails
of standing by the side of the bed,

getting down all the information
about what feels right and new,

the difference and the overlap

NEW WORDS 1939–1945

abstractionism

ack ack

activate

ad lib

air condition

angledozer

aspect ratio

autarky

automatism

baloney

barbiturate

Bauhaus

bazooka

beano

belay

bibliography

bingo

biological warfare

bitewing

blackout

blitzkrieg

blood bank

bobby pin

boondoggle

boysenberry

Brown Shirt

bulldozer

bunker

calypso

chain reaction

collage

commando

concentration camp

conga

constructivism

corny

coronary thrombosis

counterintelligence

dead pan

decontaminate

degauss

de Stijl

diorama

disqualify

documentary

double talk

electronics

escapism

evacuee

evolutionary

exhibitionism

existentialism

eye rhyme

facsimile (fax)

fascism

feather cut

feminize

Fiberglas

fink

firepower

floor show

fluorescent

foxhole

frequency modulation

gaffe

Geiger counter

gin rummy

goon

green light (v)

half-track

hammer and sickle

hasenpfeffer

heartland

hypertension

jalopy

jam session

jeep

Jehovah's witnesses

jitterbug

kamikaze

kibitz

kickback

lobotomy

masculinize

means test

Melba toast

meld

Mickey Finn

microfilm

mocha

mockup

montage

mooch

motel

motorcade

mufti

naphthaleneacetic acid

nickelodeon

Nisei

nitrogen cycle

nylon

occupational therapy

oligopoly

Pakistan

palomino

panel discussion

pantywaist

parapsychology

pastrami

penicillin

phonemics

photo finish

pinball

pin-up

planetarium

plutonium

polio

polystyrene

porkpie hat

prefabricate

pressure group

pressurize

preview

progesterone

public domain

public relations

punch drunk

quickie

racism

radar

r-colored

the real McCoy

reefer

relocation

retread

rhumba

riboflavin

roman fleuve

Rorschach test

sabotage

sadism

Sanforized

schlemiel

scorched earth

screwball

Securities and Exchange Commission

Selective Service System

semantics

Shangri-La

sharecropper

shellacking

silicone

skivvies

smorgasbord

snafu

soap opera

social credit

socialize

Social Security Act

softball

sortie

sprung rhythm

SS

Stakhanovism

Sten gun

stereophonic

steroid

streamlined

strikebreaking

striptease

submachine gun

sukiyaki

sulfanilamide

supernova

supersonic

swastika

task force

taxi dancer

Tennessee Valley Authority

testosterone

test pilot

think piece

tommy gun

tonkin

touch football

trace element

tutu

United Nations

unreconstructed

upchuck

vernacular

Volkswagen

WAC

wacky

walkie-talkie

war of nerves

Weimar republic

whodunit

wishful thinking

witch hunt

Works Progress Administration

zoot suit

ACKNOWLEDGMENTS

These poems have appeared in the following publications:

1913: "Keep the Drums at Your Mom's"

American Poetry Review: "Mostly Read the Luna Moth"

The Awl: "Otters"

Boston Review: "When I Was the Subject"

Brooklyn Rail: "My Twin"

Coconut: "Drone"

Court Green: "Twenty Blocks"

Fence: "The Throat," "Shell Game"

The Nation: "Narragansett"

New England Review: "A Million Random Digits,"
"Ha Ha Only Serious," "From the Twentieth Floor"

Northwest Review: "Feeling Numb"

Octopus: "New Words 1939–1945"

Open Letters Monthly: "Look Down"

Passages North: "The Shouting" and "The Idea Itself"

Poetry: "Ira Will Not Be Attending the Meeting"

The Poker: "My Hostility"

Shampoo: "The Facility Finder"

Sixth Finch: "City As"

Washington Square: "The Moon Is Moving"

An earlier version of the poem "The Hovel"
appeared in the chapbook *Yeah, No* (Detour, 2001).

"My Orhan Veli" consists of my versions of translations by
Murat Nemet-Nejat and Talat Sait Halman of the poems
of Orhan Veli Kanık. The series appeared as a Subpoetics
Self-Publish-or-Perish chapbook in 2007. Poems from
that series appeared in *A Public Space*, *Atlanta Review*,
Baffling Combustions, *Effing Magazine*, and *Pleiades*.

"Manyoshu Blues" consists of my versions of translations
by Ralph Hodgson of poems from the Manyoshu.

"Not Nothing Never No" was printed
as Tinyside #4 by Big Game Books.

"New Words 1939–1945" appears in the *Webster's
New Universal Unabridged Dictionary*, 1979.

EDGE BOOKS

PRIMITIVE STATE Anselm Berrigan $16 □ *SOME NOTES ON MY PROGRAMMING* Anselm Berrigan $16 □ *ZERO STAR HOTEL* Anselm Berrigan $16 □ *INTEGRITY & DRAMATIC LIFE* Anselm Berrigan $10 □ *ONCE UPON A NEOLIBERAL ROCKET BADGE* Jules Boykoff $14 □ *THE ACCORDION REPERTOIRE* Franklin Bruno $16 □ *CIPHER/CIVILIAN* Leslie Bumstead $14 □ *THE GOLDEN AGE OF PARAPHERNALIA* Kevin Davies $18 □ *COMP.* Kevin Davies $16 □ *AMERICAN WHATEVER* Tim Davis $12 □ *THE JULIA SET* Jean Donnelly $5 □ *TACHYCARDIA* Buck Downs $15 □ *LADIES LOVE OUTLAWS* Buck Downs $5 □ *MARIJUANA SOFTDRINK* Buck Downs $11 □ *CLEARING WITHOUT REVERSAL* Cathy Eisenhower $14 □ *WORLD PREFIX* Harrison Fisher $6 □ *METROPOLIS XXX: THE DECLINE & FALL OF THE ROMAN EMPIRE* Rob Fitterman $14 □ *METROPOLIS 16-20* Rob Fitterman $6 □ *ONE HUNDRED ETUDES* Benjamin Friedlander $16 □ *DICK CHENEY'S HEART* Heather Fuller $15 □ *DOVECOTE* Heather Fuller $14 □ *PERHAPS THIS IS A RESCUE FANTASY* Heather Fuller $14 □ *FLARF: AN ANTHOLOGY OF FLARF* Gardner, Gordon, Mesmer, Mohammad, & Sullivan eds. $30 □ *FLARF ORCHESTRA* (audio cd) Drew Gardner $12.99 □ *TERMINAL HUMMING* K. Lorraine Graham $15 □ *NON/FICTION* Dan Gutstein $14 □ *SIGHT* Lyn Hejinian and Leslie Scalapino $15 □ *LATE JULY* Gretchen Johnsen $4 □ *MANNERISM* Deirdre Kovac $16 *forthcoming* □ *MONSTERS* K. Silem Mohammad $16 *forthcoming* □ *DEER HEAD NATION* K. Silem Mohammad $16 *forthcoming* □ *BREATHALYZER* K. Silem Mohammad $15 □ *THE SENSE RECORD* Jennifer Moxley $14 □ *HETERONOMY* Chris Nealon $18 □ *PLUMMET* Chris Nealon $16 □

I GOOGLE MYSELF Mel Nichols $16 *forthcoming* ▢ *CATALYTIC EXTERIORIZATION PHENOMENA* Mel Nichols $16 ▢ *STEPPING RAZOR* A. L. Nielsen $9 ▢ *STRUCTURE FROM MOTION* Tom Raworth $15 ▢ *CALLER AND OTHER PIECES* Tom Raworth $12.50 ▢ *ACE* Tom Raworth $14 ▢ *DOGS* Phyllis Rosenzweig $5 ▢ *INTERVAL* Kaia Sand $14 ▢ *CROW* Rod Smith, Leslie Bumstead, eds. $10 ▢ *CUSPS* Chris Stroffolino $4 ▢ *LONG TERM RAISIN* Ryan Walker $15 ▢ *FELONIES OF ILLUSION* Mark Wallace $15 ▢ *HAZE: ESSAYS POEMS PROSE* Mark Wallace $14 ▢ *NOTHING HAPPENED AND BESIDES I WASN'T THERE* Mark Wallace $12.00 ▢ *THIS CAN'T BE LIFE* Dana Ward $18

AERIAL MAGAZINE EDITED BY ROD SMITH
AERIAL 10: Lyn Hejinian co-edited by Jen Hofer $30
AERIAL 9: Bruce Andrews $16
AERIAL 8: Barrett Watten $40
AERIAL 6/7: featuring John Cage $30

Literature published by *AERIAL/EDGE* is available through Small Press Distribution (1-800-869-7553) or from the publisher at PO Box 25642, Georgetown Station, Washington, DC 20027. When ordering from Aerial/Edge directly, add $2 postage for individual titles. Two or more titles postpaid. For more information please visit our website at www.aerialedge.com.